PARENTS

MEMORY BOOK

A DO-IT-YOURSELF AUTOBIOGRAPHY

ONE•FAM

www.onefam.com

Your Family Story

Founded in 2016, OneFam is the easy way to discover, preserve and relive your family history anywhere anytime. OneFam aims to make family history available to as many families as possible. Our suite of products include Journals, Family Tree Software (web, mobile and desktop), Ancestry DNA Testing and Family History Research. Connect, share and protect your family history for generations to come.

Visit us at onefam.com

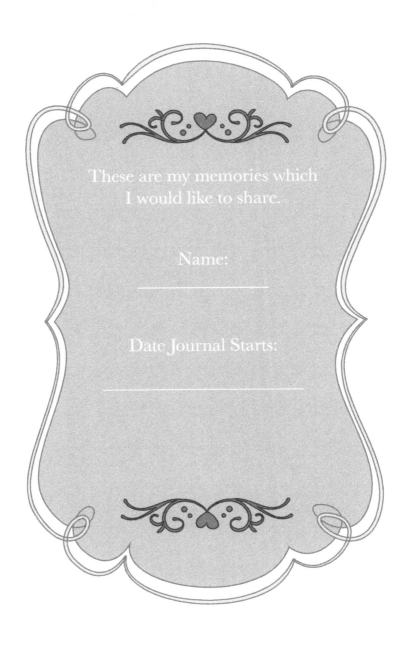

These are my memories which
I would like to share.

Name:

_____

Date Journal Starts:

_____

Table of Contents

Introduction

Whether you are 19 or 90, or somewhere in between, each of us has a story to tell; your life's story!

Imagine a world in which everyone looked the same, each person experienced the same exact journey in life and felt the same emotions! What would be the point!

That is NOT the world we live in, but rather, one filled with excitement and tragedy, joy and disappointment, hard-work and passivity, successes and failures….and varying flavors! Your life and your story is worth writing and sharing!

Everything about you is unique to the one and only YOU! Why not share with the world, or even just your loved ones, everything about what has made you and your life significant or share the journey that your family has taken throughout history!

If you are contemplating writing an autobiography, let's first consider WHY!

Ignore the haters who will ask "what makes your life interesting and worthy to be written about?" Close your ears to those who laugh at your idea. Instead, relish in the fact that whatever your reason for wanting to document your life, it is YOURS and no one can take that away from you.

- Are you looking to share your story, inspire others and make an impact?
- Do you want to document your genealogy and understand your family history?
- Have you experienced something that you would like to share with the world?
- Will this book become your legacy to pass on to future generations?

Whatever your motivation for wanting to write your autobiography, remember that it is uniquely YOU, from YOUR point of view, with your details and facts and filled with YOUR feelings and emotions.

Once you have decided to begin documenting your story, the process can be overwhelming and in fact, difficult. To guide you and help you to develop a detailed, blueprint of your history and journey, follow the prompts outlined in this book. The prompts have been divided into sections to assist you to gather your thoughts and experiences into chronological order, using your own voice, capturing the essence of the moment, including:

- Your family history (grandparents/parents)
- Birth/Early childhood
- Grade school/high school
- Post-high school/college
- Career
- Relationships
- Family
- Personal; and
- Religion

Use each section according to your ultimate goal for the finished work. If you are interested in documenting your family tree, complete as many details about your grandparents, parents and extended family as possible. Some of the prompts may be used to spark a memory or additional information from your relatives, something that you may not have originally thought of. For example, ask your mother what she remembers about how her grandparents met or what they did for a living, bringing additional insight into your family's history.

If your story relates to an experience that impacted your life, the family and personal sections may be more useful to gather your thoughts, the details of the event or circumstances and accurately document for the reader. For example, if you are sharing how you rose to the level of CEO of a major company, utilize the post-high school and career sections to gather your information and outline your book.

As you read and respond to each question, you will develop a clear picture of your life as only you could have seen it, through your eyes. From every detail about your childhood, to the challenges and decisions that have brought you to this point in your life, describe for the reader exactly how you have experienced your world. Not every question may apply to you or your life's story. However, by giving each prompt some thought, you may find yourself adding more details or information than you had originally considered.

Following the prompts and documenting your life's story will lead you down a new, and possibly unchartered path. The process, although you may have an end in mind, may also bring unintentional benefits along with it. It may be therapeutic or cause you to be retrospective. It may be the answer to a problem or the solution may be brought to light. Writing your autobiography may even bring relief or reconciliation.

Now that you have used this book to guide you to creating your finished work, what is the next step?
- Gift it to family and friends as a keepsake heirloom
- Self-publish or follow a traditional book publishing route
- Blog about it on the Internet to share with and inspire others
- Continue to add more stories in a journal for your own personal recollection and memories
- Maybe this will be the start of journaling with a loved one or child to share thoughts and questions (try one of our other journals to assist with your prompts and suggestions)
- Celebrate the book as an accomplishment in and of itself!

Regardless of how you choose to archive your autobiography, the prompts and questions herein will enable you to chronicle major dates and events; capture details and descriptions; organize your thoughts and feelings; and document appropriately HOW you want your reader to see and understand the specifics of your world, your life.

So, take your time, enjoy the process and let the world know all about YOU!

I am writing this story because....

I am writing this story because....

My grandparents details are....
(name, date of birth, place of birth)

....

....

....

....

....

....

....

....

....

....

....

....

....

....

My grandparents immigrated from/to....

....

....

....

....

....

....

....

My grandparents worked as....

My grandparents were born into wealth/poverty....

I knew/did not know my grandparents.

My grandparents school achievements included....

Details of my grandparents siblings (Father side) include....
(name, date of birth, place of birth)

Details of my grandparents siblings (Mother side) include....
(name, date of birth, place of birth)

My grandparents children's names included....

My grandparents on each side passed away at the age of....
(Or) They are still living and they are .... old.

I have the following memories of my grandparents....

I did not have a chance to ask my grandparents....

A story to remember....

A story to remember....

My parents details are....
(name, date of birth, place of birth)

. . . .
. . . .
. . . .
. . . .
. . . .
. . . .
. . . .
. . . .
. . . .
. . . .

Details of my parents siblings....
(name, date of birth, place of birth)

. . . .
. . . .
. . . .
. . . .
. . . .
. . . .
. . . .
. . . .

My parents are the oldest/youngest/middle child....

My parents grew up in....

The story of how my parents met....

My grandparents school achievements included....

My parents worked as....

During their lifetime, my parents were offered/provided some special opportunities....

My parents lived....

During their lifetime, the following events occurred in
the world....

Each of my parents was uniquely special to me because....

As far as parenting style and/or discipline, my parents were....

My most vivid parents of my parents growing up were....

I wish I knew .... about my parents.

PARENTS

The role that my mom/dad played in our house was....

My biggest supporter/champion was....

My parents' hobbies and interests include....

The characteristic that my mom/dad has that makes her/him stand out are....

My parents are/are not still alive....

Today, my relationship with my parents is....

The impact that my upbringing has had on my life is....

The most important lesson that I learned from my mother is....

The most important lesson that I learned from my father is....

A story to remember....

A story to remember....

I was born on date/location....

The name I was given was because....

My nickname was....

Growing up, I lived....

How I remember my childhood home....

A story my parents told be about my birth/early childhood....

My sibling details are....
(name, date of birth, place of birth)

I do not have any siblings, and being an only child has impacted my life....

My siblings and I typically argued about....

My relationship with my siblings is… It has/has not changed since we were children.

My earliest memory is....

My playmates as a child were....

My first friend was....

The most influential person in my life when I was young was....

My favourite recipe from childhood was....

During school breaks/summertime, I....

My most memorable birthday was....

At bedtime/nighttime, our routine was....

. . . .
. . . .
. . . .
. . . .
. . . .
. . . .
. . . .
. . . .
. . . .

When I was young, I was afraid of....

. . . .
. . . .
. . . .
. . . .
. . . .
. . . .
. . . .
. . . .
. . . .

I received a gift from .... and it meant so much to me because....

A typical family vacation was....

When I was a toddler/elementary school, I once....

The object that I still treasure from my childhood is....

I felt most fulfilled/happy when....

The one thing I am most proud of as a young child is....

I am most like my (which parent) ....

I enjoyed/did not enjoy school....

My favorite subject in school was....

I liked most/least at school....

Learning was difficult/easy for me....

My teachers used to tell my parents....

As a child, when I grew up, I wanted to be a....

I worked part-time at....

When I earned money, I used it for....

The thing I learned as a child which impacted my financial life as an adult was....

My first car was....

As a child, I participated in the following sports....

If I were to describe myself academically, I would say I was....

My favorite teacher in school was....

Outside of school, I enjoyed....

If I were to describe myself socially during high school, I would say I was....

When I was in high school, band/music/dance was popular....

My most fond memory from high school was....

I volunteered at....

The person that I most admired during high school was....

During high school, the most important thing I learned about myself was....

My high school education prepared me/did not prepare me for college/career....

Of my friends from high school, I still remain in contact with….

I attended my 5/10/20 year reunion....

When I was in high school, the following occurred in the world....

If I could speak to my 15-year-old self, I would tell him/her....

A story to remember....

A story to remember....

I attended college/university/trade school at....

I lived on campus/commuted....

I chose/wanted to study…. because….

I decided to/not to go to college because....

My closest friend in college was....

This friend influenced me by....

I am/am not satisfied with the education that I received during college because....

. . . .

. . . .

. . . .

. . . .

. . . .

. . . .

. . . .

. . . .

. . . .

If I had to do it all over again, I would change....

. . . .

. . . .

. . . .

. . . .

. . . .

. . . .

. . . .

. . . .

. . . .

. . . .

My most vivid memory from college was....

I enlisted in the military because....

I served in the military.... My responsibilities included....

I chose to tell my family that I enlisted on/at....

My military service was an important time in my life because....

My college/military service helped to shape my future career....

During this time, the most important thing I learned about myself was....

My role model was....

During my college years, when I was not in class, I....

My college education prepared me/did not prepare me for my future career.

I developed a very close relationship with....
(list college friends and provide details)

I still remain in contact with....

A story to remember....

A story to remember....

My first job after college was....

I got my first job through…. It was/was not in my field of study.

I truly felt grown up when....

My first paycheck was for....

My first job did/did not meet my expectations of what I envisioned doing after college.

If I had to describe my work ethic, I would say....

My ideal job/career is....

I have/have not experienced the ideal job.

The person who has most influenced me in my career is....

This person impacted my life by....

I have had…. Number of jobs to this point in my life.

I enjoy my line of work because…It does/does not give me personal satisfaction?

Outside of work, I enjoy....

I also work as....

I define "success" as....

My ultimate career goal is....

CAREER

When working I feel valued and appreciated because....

My job has granted me opportunities/rewards....

I hope to retire when.... or I already retired at age....

CAREER

After leaving the work world, I plan on....

During retirement, I hope to accomplish something I have never done before....

CAREER

If you could change anything about my career choice, it would be....

I am not working in my original career because....

In terms of my career, my greatest challenge has been....

My biggest regret about my career is....

A story to remember....

My first love was....

I am married to/in a partnership with….(give details)

We have been together/married for….

I met my spouse/partner at....

When my children marry, the most important thing I could tell them about marriage and relationships is....

The most important/special thing about our relationship is....

The most significant that has happened during our
relationship is....

We usually disagree about....

To earn a living, my spouse....

If I had to describe our marriage/partnership, I would say....

We used to enjoy...... but no longer do this together because....

We now enjoying doing .... together....

I have always looked for this qualities in a partner....

I most admire this quality in my spouse/partner....

Some problems existed in our relationship because....

My best friend is....(give details)

He/she has been in my life since....

The thing/secret that I have shared with my best friend but not my spouse is....

The quality that I most value in others is....

A story to remember....

A story to remember....

I have …. number of children. (name, gender, date of birth, place of birth).

With the birth of each of my children, I was changed....

My goal as a parent has always been....

FAMILY

I do not have children because…. or I plan on having children in the future….

I can describe my parenting style as.... This is the same/
different from how my children would describe it.

Some things I specifically do in parenting is due to how I was raised by my parents. These include....

In my home, I have the role of....

My greatest dream/expectation for my children is....

FAMILY

The bad qualities in me that I hope to not pass on to my children are....

The good qualities in me which I hope to pass on to my children are....

I hope to pass on our family tradition of …. to my children/
grandchildren?

The thing that makes our family unique is....

The most difficult thing I find about raising children is....

I have told my children a little white lie about....

A story to remember....

A story to remember....

I am most passionate about....

PERSONAL

The thing that makes me get out of bed every day is....

I define happiness as....

The accomplishment I am most proud of in my life is....

The greatest challenge in my life has been....

I want to leave as my Legacy....

I want to be remembered as....

The scariest thing that has ever happened to me was....

My greatest fear is....

My most embarrassing most was....

My favorite book is…. It impacted my life….

I have a bad habit of....

PERSONAL

My biggest pet peeve is....

If I could go back in time and change one moment or event, it would be....

I have traveled outside the country to…My favorite vacation location is….

My favorite food is....

An event that helped to shape my life was....

There are some contradictions or ironies in my life including....

If I had more time in my day, I would....

The thing that is missing in my life is....

The characteristic in others that is most annoying to me is....

The thing that I regret doing most in my life is....

I lost a person close to me. This loss impacted my life....

The thing that has significantly changed the trajectory of my life is....

I have significantly impacted someone else's life by....

The quality that makes me different or unique is....

If I could change one thing about myself, it would be....

The main lesson that I have learned in life so far is....

My personal mantra or rule that I live by is....

. . . .

. . . .

. . . .

. . . .

. . . .

. . . .

. . . .

. . . .

The message that I want to relay to others is....

. . . .

. . . .

. . . .

. . . .

. . . .

. . . .

. . . .

. . . .

. . . .

. . . .

. . . .

My life's purpose is....

If I could go back in time, I would live in the following time period....because....

One thing that I have done that is outside my comfort zone is....

PERSONAL

One thing I wish I had done differently....

The best time period of my life was....

PERSONAL

The worst time of my life was....

A defining moment occurred in my life when....

PERSONAL

My life experience has prepared me for my career/book/next phase of life by....

I laugh when....

I cry when....

An event that helped to shape my life was....

My hero is....

A famous quote that most defines me is....

The one word that my friends would use to describe me is....

The tough questions that I ask myself every day include....

My "Bucket List" includes....

PERSONAL

Sometimes I question my existence and my purpose because....

I am most grateful for....

In the next 10/20 years, I see myself....

The things that are important to me that have changed over the
years include....

The thing I value most in my life is....

A story to remember....

A story to remember....

My religious affiliation is....

I define spirituality as....

The thing that has most impacted my belief system?

I believe that God has a plan for my life because....

Religion impacted my life by....

My religious beliefs have changed since I was young because....

The role that religion played when I was young was....

My belief system has helped/hindered my life because....

When I die, I expect to....

I have or need to forgive someone who has hurt me....

If I could see one person again, it would be....

When I meet God, I want to ask him....

My beliefs and wishes....

My beliefs and wishes....

Sign Up to OneFam

At OneFam we aim to make family history available to everyone. We would like to invite you to become a member of OneFam community and enjoy exclusive benefits. With already over 25,000 users worldwide, we promise you'll be in good company.

- **50%** off your next journal purchases
- **A**ccess to free family tree software
- **B**irthday gifts
- **F**ree shipping offers
- **F**irst dibs on sales
- & more...

To subscribe, simply visit our website at:

https://www.onefam.com/subscribe/

Create Your Family Free

Get started with your free online family tree in minutes. Simply sign up, add your parents, siblings, children, grandparents and other family members.

- Preserve Images, Videos, Audio, Stories & Events
- Invite & Connect with Family Members
- Create and Share Family History
- Available on Web, Mobile and Ipad

More Great Journals

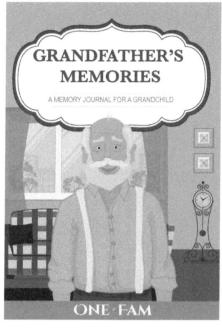

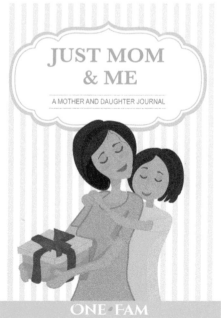

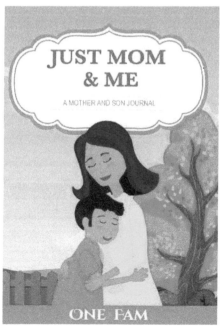

Visit Onefam.com for our full range